Help!

I've been asked to officiate

a Wedding Ceremony!

by Antoinette Marold

Dedication

In remembrance of my mother...

Mary Kubala Slovensky Vasso

Introduction

This book is a guide for officiants and the couples who have decided to ask a friend or family member to officiate their wedding ceremony.

Within these pages, it is my hope that you will find all the information that you will need to have a beautiful, meaningful marriage ceremony.

Table of Contents

For the Couple & Officiant:

Congratulations on your upcoming marriage.

I hope you will give time and thought to planning your marriage ceremony.

Take the time to discuss your feelings regarding the ceremony, what you want to say to each other, and what you want your guests to remember about your ceremony. This should be a meaningful event in your lives.

Your officiant should be able to guide you through and coordinate the entire ceremony.

We are living in a changing world and some changes are also taking place regarding wedding ceremonies.

We still have the white dress.

We still have the tuxedo. However, the formal tux is sometimes becoming a suit. (Very nice seeing that most weddings do not require a formal attire.)

We still have bouquets and boutonnières.

We still have rings. (usually double ring ceremonies)

We still have a parent or parents walking the bride or couple down the aisle.

We still have wedding parties.

We still have photographers and music.

Bridal veils….not so much.

Church weddings….not as much.

Aisle runners….not so much.

Some updates and changes:

Elaborate engagement proposals. Very public.

The person who can legally officiate a marriage ceremony.

If legal in their state, some couples are requesting a friend or family member to officiate their wedding ceremony.

Venues have expanded.

This book is being written as a guide for officiants and couples who are bypassing the professional officiants.

For the Couple

Are you thinking about asking a friend or family member to officiate your wedding ceremony? Following are some questions that you may want to ask yourself before you make your final decision.

What are your reasons for asking this particular person to officiate your wedding?

Is this person comfortable speaking in front of a large/ small group of people?

Are they well organized?
Are they dependable?
Are they creative?
Can they coordinate your ceremony?
Can they guide you through the ceremony process?
Can they guide your wedding party through the processional at the ceremony etc.?
Can they coordinate a rehearsal?
Are they legally authorized to officiate a wedding?
Can you depend on them to sign the proper documents and send them to the proper place to meet civil requirements?

Will they be responsible for the officiant's copy of your marriage documents?

If you think that the planning of your ceremony is not going as you had hoped, would you be able to verbalize your feelings or change your officiant?

For the Officiant

You have been asked by friends or family to officiate their wedding. Following are some things to think about before you accept.

Are you comfortable officiating this marriage ceremony?

How well do you know this couple? Do you know them too well?

If you sense a problem, would you be comfortable recommending they see a marriage counselor?

Are you willing to seek out information on officiating a wedding ceremony?

It is important for you to check with your state, county, and or city, on the officiant requirements. You may be required to get a license. In that event, it may require ordination.

If you are getting ordained online, keep a record of the organization.

Are you calm in a crisis?

Are you an organized person?

Can you coordinate a ceremony including the music, reviewing the ceremony with musicians and the photographer?

Chapter 1

First Meeting

Couple

You are having your first meeting with the person who is not a professional but who is going to preside (officiate) at your wedding ceremony.

Following are a few ways that you can help to prepare for a successful meeting.

Take with you the following information:

Ceremony date and time
Ceremony venue and address
Venue contact person
Wedding Party names
Readers names (if you decide to have readings)
Musicians names
Photographer names
Immediate family names

Discuss between yourselves the vision you have for your ceremony.

Are you planning on a wedding theme?

Check on marriage license information.

Will you be offering a payment for the officiant's services? It is best to handle this question at the first meeting, as it prevents misunderstandings.

Officiant

On the first meeting with the couple, it is best to be well prepared.

The questions about the couple on the Information page will be very helpful in planning the ceremony.

Gathering their venue, family, and ceremony preferences is very important and will keep you well informed. Sample forms follow.

It is important to ask the questions regarding type of ceremony they would like to plan. Will the ceremony have a theme?

It would be very helpful if you do some research on ceremony openings, readings, and vows.

This is also the time to discuss a fee if you are expecting one.

Chapter 2

Information Forms

Wedding Ceremony Couple Information Sheet

Bride/ Partner:

____Marriages:________

Address:____________________City:__________St: ___Zip:______

E-mail:____

Phone Home:________________Cell:____________________

Children?_______Names:______________________________

Parents:____

Brothers: Sisters:

Maternal Grandparents: Paternal Grandparents :

Groom/Partner:

____Marriages:________

Address:____________________City:__________St :___Zip:______

E-mail:____

Phone Home:________________Cell:____________________

Children?____Names:__________________________________

Parents:____

Brothers: Sisters:

Maternal Grandparents: Paternal Grandparents:

Ceremony Date:______________Ceremony Time:__________________

Location:____

Lic. Issued in what county:________________Number Guests:______

Rehearsal
Date:________Time:________Location:____________________

Along with the information sheet, things you should be looking for:

Are either of the couples parents divorced?
Are they remarried?
Is their relationship with each other friendly?
If they are remarried will their spouse be attending?
If applicable what is their relationship with the couples?

Review the grandparents and their marriage status.

Will the parents be seated formally? As part of the entrance processional?

Will the Bride (or Partner) be escorted to the ceremony area? If yes, by whom? Will there be an aisle runner?

Will there be a wedding party? How many?
Any children in the wedding party?

Ask for their names.
Ask the children's ages.

If you can, at this first meeting, ask for the names of the wedding party and how they will be partnered.

Additional Information.....

Will the couple be seeing each other before the ceremony?

Is the Wedding Venue - Indoors or out?
If it is outdoors, is there a rain venue?

Will there be musicians for the ceremony? Names.

Will there be a sound system? A microphone for the officiant?

If the couple is hesitating about having a sound system, especially outdoors, try to convince them of the importance of their guests being able to hear the ceremony.

Will there be a professional photographer?

If the couple is not planning on having professionals (music, photographer etc.), encourage them to have a boom box /i tunes for music and inquire who will be in charge of the music and who will be taking the photos.

It is important to review the service with both the musicians and photographers on the day of the ceremony.

It is also good to have ushers to seat the guests.
Ushers do not have to be in the wedding party.
If there is a large wedding party, and a lot of guests, both the men and women of the wedding party can be ushers.

Once you know the number of guests, you will know how many ushers you will need. One for every 50 guests.

Chapter 3

The Processional

Wedding Party Processional

Prelude Music

Seating of the Grandparents ☐ yes   ☐ no

Groom/Partner
Paternal Grandparents

____

Maternal Grandparents

____

Bride/Partner
Paternal Grandparents

____

Maternal Grandparents

____

Seating of the parents   ☐ yes ☐ no

Parents of the Groom/Partner

____

Additional Parents of the Groom/Partner

____

Parents of the Bride/Partner

____

Additional Parents of the Bride/Partner

____

After the grandparents are seated, the officiant usually enters the ceremony. Most often the officiant precedes the groom/partner down the aisle. Or perhaps from the front left side of the ceremony area.

You may want to process down the aisle and turn around to the face the guests, then the groom/partner would process down the aisle.

Or you may want to be the very first person to enter (before grandparents are seated).

If the grandparents were seated before the officiant, they can be coached as to when to start down the aisle.

Notes:

Wedding Party Processional (cont'd)

MUSIC FOR THE WEDDING PARTY

Groom/Partner & Bestman/Usher

____

or will the Bestman/Usher be entering with his wedding party partner?

If Groomsmen/Ushers are entering single file, they would enter first, then the Bridesmaids/Attendants. If the couples are processing together, the Bestman/Usher could enter with the Groom/Partner or enter with the Maid of Honor/Attendant

Groomsmen/Ushers

____

____

____

____

Bridesmaids/Attendants

____

____

____

____

____

Maid of Honor/Attendant

____

Children

____

____

____

MUSIC FOR THE BRIDE/Partner
Bride/Partner Escorted by:

____

Chapter 4

The Ceremony

Wedding Party Processional

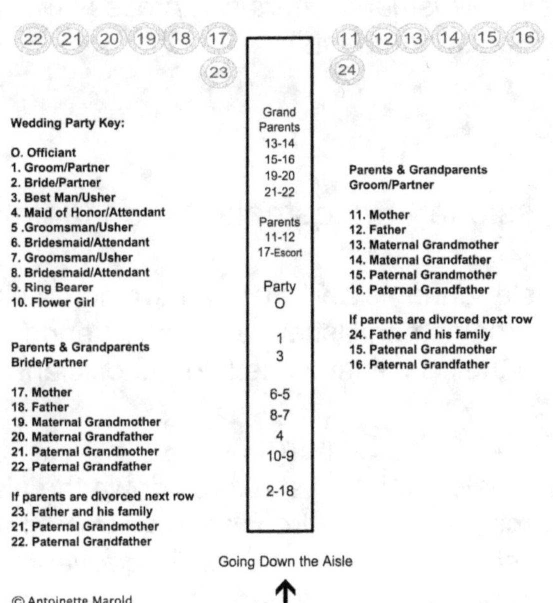

Wedding Party Key:

O. Officiant
1. Groom/Partner
2. Bride/Partner
3. Best Man/Usher
4. Maid of Honor/Attendant
5. Groomsman/Usher
6. Bridesmaid/Attendant
7. Groomsman/Usher
8. Bridesmaid/Attendant
9. Ring Bearer
10. Flower Girl

Parents & Grandparents
Bride/Partner

17. Mother
18. Father
19. Maternal Grandmother
20. Maternal Grandfather
21. Paternal Grandmother
22. Paternal Grandfather

If parents are divorced next row
23. Father and his family
21. Paternal Grandmother
22. Paternal Grandfather

Parents & Grandparents
Groom/Partner

11. Mother
12. Father
13. Maternal Grandmother
14. Maternal Grandfather
15. Paternal Grandmother
16. Paternal Grandfather

If parents are divorced next row
24. Father and his family
15. Paternal Grandmother
16. Paternal Grandfather

Going Down the Aisle

↑

Prelude Music
Seating of Grandparents

Seating of Parents
If the mothers are lighting candles or bringing sand, etc., it would be done at this time as part of the processional.

Entrance of Officiant
Entrance of Groom/Partner & Groomsmen/Ushers
(or the Groomsmen/Ushers can process with the Bridesmaids/Attendants)

Music

Processional- Bridesmaids/Attendants

If an aisle runner is being used, it would be placed by 1 or 2 Groomsmen/Ushers after the Attendants have reached their destination next to the officiant.

Children
If rose petals are being scattered down the aisle by one or more of the children, it is best to put the runner down first. Aisle runners are no longer very popular because they can be slippery.

Officiant asks the guests to stand.

Music
Processional for the Bride/Partner and Escort

Bride/Partner escorted by: Could be Father, or Mother, both Parents, or a special family member or friend.

The Groom/Partner can also be escorted by his parents or the couple process down the aisle together, especially if there are no parents in attendance or if they have been married before.

When the couple is in front of you, the officiant, you can ask "Who gives this women/person to be married?" This is not required. It is best not to ask the couple if it is something that they would like to add because the custom comes from a time when women were property and given in marriage.

But…If the couple insist, it is their wedding!

The couple are now facing you.

OPENING OR GREETING

This is the time that you would welcome guests to the wedding ceremony. You could introduce yourself at this time as well. Example: "Good Afternoon. Welcome to the wedding ceremony of Betty and John ,"or you can use their full names.

You can also express the feelings of the couple. Example:
"Betty and John are so happy that you are here to celebrate their marriage."

If you are introducing yourself and you are a friend or family, you may also want to express your feelings regarding being invited to officiate this marriage ceremony.

You can end this segment by reading a prayer. Or you can also acknowledge those who were not able to be present at the ceremony.

ADDRESSING THE COUPLE

Prepare a short message to the couple regarding love or marriage. This would also be the time to explain the wedding theme if one has been planned.

READINGS

Two readings are usually included. Ask the couple to select family or friend to read the readings.

Invite the first reader to come forward and read the selected reading.

The same for the second reader.

You can separate the readings with music or perhaps a quote.

Be sure to have a copy of the readings. Bring an extra copy for the reader as well. If the couple emails a copy of the readings to the readers before the wedding day, it is a great help. Hopefully they will rehearse their segment of the ceremony.

Now with the world wide web at our fingertips, there are huge selections of poetry, prayers, verses, etc. to select from for the ceremony.   These readings are usually selected by the couple.

OFFICIANT ADDRESS

This is where you, as officiate, address the couple and the guests with a very brief comment on Love and/or Marriage. Keeping in mind, that if you are out of doors or in a venue where the couple is going to remain standing during the entire ceremony, you want to keep it brief.

A caution to you regarding this segment of the ceremony: there is a danger of knowing the couple too well. Do not get too personal.

Sharing the following example:
I was a guest at a wedding ceremony where the couple asked their two friends, who were pastors of a small house church,(but who did not have opportunities to officiate weddings), to officiate their marriage ceremony.

When it came time for the officiants to address the group, they became very personal. It seems that the couple had some problems during their courtship and the officiants decided to tell the guests about their problems. It was terrible. Guests were fidgeting in their seats, the couple as well as the guests were embarrassed, and it seemed that no amount of shocked looks caused the officiants to end their stories.

There may be some funny stories that you have about the couple but keep it for the rehearsal dinner. Or the stories may not even be appropriate at that time.

CONSENT, VOWS, PRONOUNCEMENT

The next three segments are referred to as the Rite of Marriage especially in a religious ceremony. They are most important and necessary segments of the ceremony. Consent and Pronouncement are the necessary legal segments of the ceremony.

CONSENT

You must ask them for their Consent:

Steven and Michelle, (couple's names)
you have come together in the
presence of this community.
I ask you to state your intentions.

Have you come here freely and without reservation to give yourselves to each other in marriage? (couple answers "Yes)"

Will you love and honor each other as husband and wife for the rest of your lives? (or Partners)
(couple answers "I will")

If you want to change the words you certainly can, but however you decide to address the subject, it must be Consent.

VOWS

There are traditional vows with the officiant reciting the vows and the couple answering: "I do."

If the couple decides on traditional vows, try to persuade them to repeat the vows after you so that they are actually saying the vows,

Groom/Partner is first:

"I Steven, take you Michelle, to be my wedded wife.
To have and to hold, from this day forward.
For better, for worse, for richer, for poorer.
In sickness and in health, to love and to cherish,
As long as we both shall live."

You can also say "until death I do part", but many prefer "as long as we both shall live" better.

Bride/Partner repeats. Of course using her name first and "husband" instead of "wife".

You can also use "Do you take________to be your partner?"

The vows can be very creative. The couple can write their own vows. There are many samples of vows on the internet. Include selecting their vows part of their homework along with selecting music and readings.

The vow sharing is not mandatory. The couple does not have to recite identical vows.

RING EXCHANGE

You can introduce the rings:

Example:

These rings, like the love you share, have no beginning or end. They are outward and visible signs of an inward and spiritual quality of life and love, signifying to all the bond of marriage you share.

RING BLESSING

If the couple would like their wedding rings blessed, the blessing is before the exchange.

RING EXCHANGE

One of the most used ring exchanges is:

Starting with the Groom/Partner

"Michelle, with this ring I thee wed.
I pledge you my love and fidelity."

Bride/Partner follows with the same wording.

The couple can also write their own ring exchange.

Sometimes couples have decided to recite their vows and ring exchanges extemporaneously. It usually does not work out well.

If the couple has a theme: Lighting candles, pouring sand, pouring wine, rose presentation to each other or to mothers, it is done at this time. Wording for themes can be found on the internet.

PRONOUNCEMENT

In most religious tradition ceremonies, the Pronouncement comes immediately after the vows. However, you can make the Pronouncement at the end of the ceremony before the introduction.

FINAL WORDS

This can be a blessing, poem or words of encouragement.

NOW IS WHEN YOU CAN PRONOUNCE THE COUPLE:

"By the power vested in me by the State of _______,
I pronounce you husband and wife (Partners)."
<u>You must pronounce the couple.</u>

THE KISS

INTRODUCTION OF COUPLE

Ask the couple what they would prefer: Mr. & Mrs. their last name, or would they like to use their first names with the joint last name.

Or would they like Partners for life and their first names.

Many couples are not changing names after they are married.

RECESSIONAL with music…

RECESSIONAL

IN THIS ORDER

Married Couple

Bestman/Usher and Maid of Honor/Attendant

Children

Wedding Party by Couples

Parents of the Bride/Partner
Parents of the Groom/Partner

Grandparents of the Bride/Partner
Grandparents of the Groom/Partner

Officiant

Will there be a receiving line?
If so here is the order.

1. Mother of the Bride/Partner
2. Father of the Bride/Partner
3. Bride/Partner
4. Groom/Partner
5. Mother of the Groom/Partner
6. Father of the Groom/Partner

The bridal party is usually not included in the
receiving line.

Officiant

SIGNING OF THE MARRIAGE CERTIFICATE

Keeping in mind that you have asked the couple for their consent and pronounced them married, you have taken care of the legal aspects of the ceremony except for the signing of the documents and filing them with the proper authorities.

Check the officiant rules of the state where you are officiating the ceremony, as to who, if anyone other than yourself, has to sign the marriage documents.

You are responsible for sending in the documents to the proper authorities. You should have a copy to keep for your records.

Send the signed documents via Certified Mail. This enables you to track them online to determine when they arrive at the Court.

Chapter 5

Readings

For the Couple and Officiant

Some favorite readings ……

Apache Wedding Blessing *by Albert Maltz*

Be Love Now *by Ram Dass*

Love is an Adventure *by Pierre Tielhart de Chardon*

Blessings for a Marriage *by James Dillet Freeman*

Excerpt fromThe Gift of the Sea *by Anne Morrow Lindbergh*

On Marriage from the Prophet *by Khalil Gibran*

Union *by Robert Fulghum*

Instructions for Life *by his holiness the 4th Dalai Lama*

To Love is Not to Possess *by James Kavanaugh*

The Privileged Lovers *by Rumi*

A Touch of Heart *by Ernie Jonas*

My True Love Hath My Heart *by Sir Philip Sidney*

Words to Live by Within Marriage *by Colin McCarty*

Yesterday, Today and Tomorrow *by Kit McCallum*

Two Trees *by Janet Miles*

And I Have You *by Nikki Giovanni*

Sonnet XLIII *by Elizabeth Barrett Browning*

See Clearly *by Lau Tzu, Tao Te Ching*

Always Return *by Lau Tzu, Tao Te Ching*

A Sacred Space *by Lau Tzu, Tao Te Ching*

I Will Be Here *by Steven Curtis Chapman*

You're The One For Me *by Dallas Fisher*

Our Love *by Bruce B. Wilmer*

Readings from the Bible…

Old Testament

Genesis 1:26-28, 3a

Genesis 2:18-24

Genesis 24:48-51; 58-67

Song of Songs 2:8-10, 14 16a; 8;6-7a

Sirach 26:1-4, 16-21

Jeremiah: 31 31-32a, 33-34a

New Testament

Romans 8:31b-35, 37-39

Romans 12:1-2, 9-12

Romans 12:1-2, 9-18

I Corinthians 6:13c-15a, 17-20

I Corinthians 12:31-13:8a

Ephesians 5:2a, 21-33

I John 4:7-12

About the Author

Antoinette is commissioned/ordained by The Federation of Christian Ministries (FCM) of which she served as Chairperson for six years, 2007-2013. She continues to be active in FCM as their Graphic Designer and Communication Chair. She is a Wedding Celebrant/Officiant and an instructor of the Online Wedding Celebrant Training Course at Global Ministries University.

She is also the author of "By the Power vested in me…" A Guide for Wedding Celebrants/Officiants Available at http://amzn.com/1495368769

Antoinette worked for many years with couples who were planning their wedding as a bridal consultant and event planner. Antoinette is also past senior member (member for ten years or more) of the Association of Bridal Consultants. She also served the wedding industry as a designer of wedding cakes and as a florist.

Antoinette can be reached at:
AMMweddings@gmail.com